Reflections: A Journey to Abundance

Michelle Wilson

Presentation by *BookLeaf Publishing*

Web: www.bookleafpub.com

E-mail: info@bookleafpub.com

ISBN: 9789358314779

First edition 2023

For Ellie, James, Isabella, Andy, Lilly & Chris.

There is always a shining light in the times of darkness.

That light is hope.

Hope is always guiding you home.

M x

ACKNOWLEDGEMENT

To the many lessons life has thrown my way,
sometimes more than once.
To the darkness and disappointment.
You didn't win.
You made me grow.
You made me evolve.
You made me love.
You made me stronger.
I thank you.
I look forward and never back.

PREFACE

It was only a matter of time before the words
would flow, but the time eventually came.
I knew I needed to document this chapter.
Grief has shaped me beyond recognition and the
person I was before simply does not exist.
The process has not been an easy road, but I
have allowed myself to think and feel.
I understand I am left with a true, authentic
version of me.
The real me.
This is my journey to abundance.

The Girl.

I will endlessly encourage.
Perpetually pursue those dreams of longing.
You are capable beyond measure; supporting to
succeed.
I will endlessly encourage you, my love.

I will offer determination.
Adversity will present an infinite barrier,
Remember, I'm possible; never impossible.
I will offer determination, my love.

I will show resilience.
Look ahead when the challenges consume; a
quiet confidence.
Be true to yourself and values.
I will show resilience, my love.

I will muster strength.
Despondency under dark days; enduring clouds
that never clear.
A warrior who knows no bounds; an unspoken
promise.
I will muster strength, my love.

I will reveal compassion.
Confusion and doubt seep through every pore.

Mistakes bring uncertainty; a lesson to teach.
I will reveal compassion, my love.

I will comfort you and wipe your tears.
Setbacks and sorrow will be frequent.
Unbearable disappointment and pain; the path
will alter.
I will comfort you and wipe your tears, my love.

I will keep you safe.
Intuition is your greatest asset; listen to the inner
voice.
Frequency and secure knowledge will guide the
way.
I will keep you safe, my love.

I will teach you gratitude.
A glimmer in the melancholy; a beacon to light
any expanse.
Positivity and infectious energy, so warming.
I will teach you gratitude, my love.

I will present you with love.
Worthy of undoubted happiness; joy and
abundance radiating.
A smile that illuminates inside, the window to
your soul.
I will present you with love, my love.

Trust me, my love.
I speak with a tranquil confidence.
You can trust me, my love.

The Sunshine.

Believe in optimism.
Believe in miracles.
Believe that magic happens.
Believe in yourself.
Believe in the impossible.
Believe in happiness.
Believe in what radiates a smile like sunshine.
That is meant for you.
That is yours.

The Memory.

Repeating and rewinding;
Consuming and evocative.

Fading is no option;
Only the gentle ebb and flow.

Reality and imagination,
Blurred as one.

Unaltered and mournful;
The outcome remains constant.

The Core.

Detached from the showcase to the outside
world; the curtain draws.
The distinct applause muffles and fades.
An intense illusion; a false confidence.

Removing the mask; a character portrayed so
effortlessly.
Differing narratives; many faces revealed.

The private audience selected; an inner sanctum.
Exposing and unveiling the layers.
Authentic and untamed; the fragile core remains.

The Friend.

She is the one with perception,
Understanding silence speaks volumes.

She is the one who is available,
A thoughtfulness for the other.

She is the one who cares,
with kindness and benevolence.

She is the one who upholds loyalty,
A motivation for compassion.

She is the one who brings honesty,
To help create peace and understanding.

She is the one who is by your side,
The friend you can trust.

The Path.

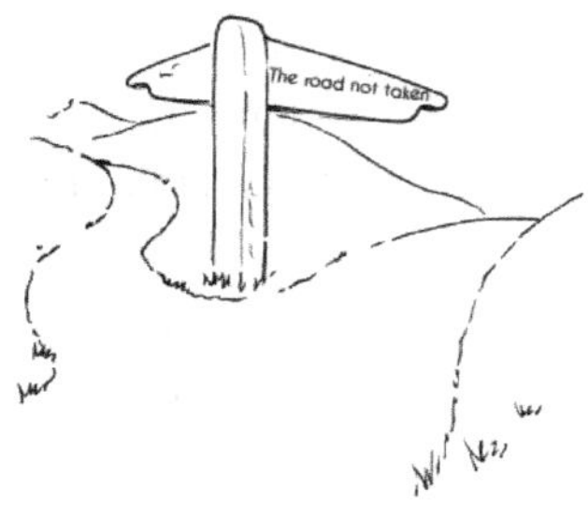

Your path is laid out.
Meandering with purpose.
Fate empowers.
The path is unpredictable.
Slow and stable.
Fast and uncertain.
Arduous struggles.
A personal choice or the path already chosen?
The way forward.
It's your choice.
Moving tentatively.
Which path do I take?
A reluctance.
But you know.
I am ready.
Sunrise on the horizon.
Your path is laid out.
Meandering with purpose.
Fate empowers.

The Soul.

Reach for the stars, with such intensity.
Release the self-doubt.
Sparkle effortlessly,
Have the courage and confidence to be resolute,
Be brave.
Go above and beyond.
Show the world you,
Release the energy and spirit,
Show up as your authentic self,
With determination and resilience.
Adventure and contentment,
Let your soul serve its purpose.

The Mirage.

In that single tear that fell so delicately, was her
sorrow;
the illusion of confidence that passes from her
lips.
The vulnerability in her eyes a mere portal;
heartbreak permeating every alcove deep inside.
A reason for her sadness.

A fragile mirage of the complex character she so
eloquently portrays.
The thrall of genuine laughter;
a glimpse of melancholy in her smile.

She is the force that can not be tamed;
determination permeating amidst the grief.

The gentle juxtaposition weaved effortlessly in
her gaze.

All but one knows her truth.
The key to unlock her inner world; soothing her
haunted soul.
Handling with compassion the grief she carries.

The Plan.

It was never part of the plan;
but it was always part of the plan.

When sadness is left scattered in ash; it settles
and stagnates.
Disappointment.

Embers glow vividly; and disperse
unpredictably.
Endurance.

A flame reignites meticulously, illuminating the
ashen terrain.
Silver lining.

Enriched with endurance; effortlessly, fertile
surroundings prevail.
Hope.

Melancholy beauty. Tainted yet undiluted; rich
authenticity.
Constant.

It was never part of the plan;
but it was always part of the plan.

The Love.

There you were, unexpected and uninvited.
A moment in time.
It will never be the same.
The tenderness of your smile.
A distinct familiarity, unexplained.
I see behind those deep eyes,
We have been here previously.
Such intensity, absorbed in intrigue.
A connection so formidable,
I know you.
Melting deeper; protected in the soothing
embrace.
Desire to develop and evolve.
A magnetism so forceful,
I am home.
A moment in time.
A chemistry so intoxicating.
It's always been you.
The path will forever be entwined,I close my
eyes and meander freely; immersed in
imagination.
Time changes nothing.
Follow your heart and you will be home.
We are one.

The Mother.

The greatest gift is a love so pure,
You are part of me.

I am changed beyond measure.
The simple touch of your hand,
overwhelming devotion.

I am blessed beyond measure.
I will take joy from your laughter,
pain from your sorrow.

You are protected beyond measure.
Your greatest support will guide and teach;
Anything is possible,
so make your dreams come true.

Never doubt my love for you,
You are loved beyond measure.
You are safe with me, your mother.

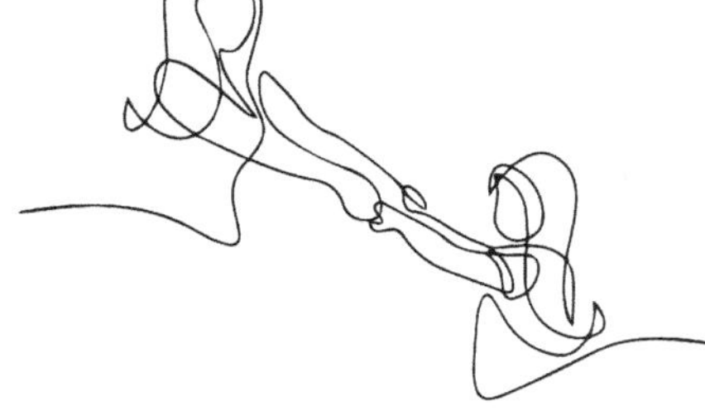

The Sadness.

It's not your time.
What is reality? For I do not know.
A heaviness.
A tiredness.
I want to sleep.
Blissful from reality.
Where am I going?
I travel away from my body.
But alas, into reverse.
The mortal realm.
I recognise her,
a haunting face imposing.
It's not your time.

The Scar.

The open wound is instantaneous;
Unexpected.
An unwanted irregularity;
Fragile.
Damage concealed deep underneath;
Permeates.
A mysterious, irregular beauty;
Imperfection.
In that imperfection is change;
Healing.
Gift of time encourages fading;
Altered.
Process of gentle care and attention;
Scarred.
Sorrow steadily seeping through;
Triggered.
Locked away secrets surface;

Flawed.
Part of me never healing fully;
Acceptance.

The Darkness.

The overwhelming sorrow, I see no light.
There is no escape from this prison.
For when love is powerful and strong,
It magnifies a pain like no other.
It knows no boundaries and limits.
A constant ache that is exacerbated and throbs.
No acceptance. No closure.

A gaping wound raw and jagged.
Constant sadness at the core.
Why did you come if only to leave?
In the morning dawn, in the evening darkness;
You are there.

There is no happy ending here.
Destined for an outcome,
where you are merely a passenger.
A moment in time that stands still,
heavy and consuming.
You are there.

The Strength.

Who is she?
I never knew. I never knew she existed.

Where did she come from?
I never knew. I never knew she was always
there.

Why is she here?
I never knew. I never knew she showed me all I
am.

What will she teach me?
I never knew. I never knew she showed me the
way forward.

Who is she?
I never knew. But I know now.

Where did she come from?
I know now. She was always there.

Why is she here?
I know now. I never chose this reality; she is my
soul awakened.

What will she teach me?

I now know. She was there when I needed her
spirit and guidance.

Who is she?
She is my strength. She is me.

The Question.

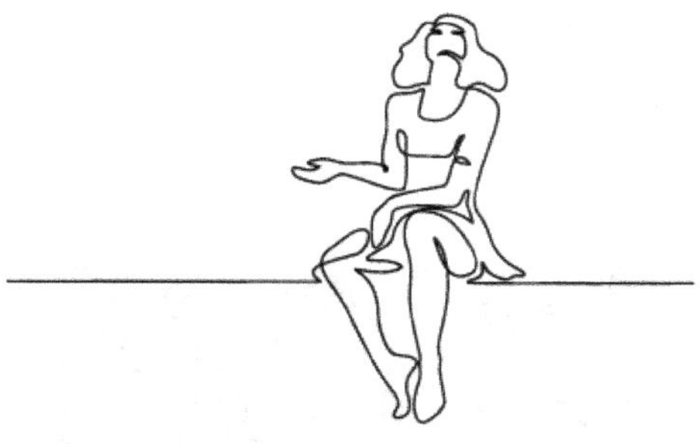

Spontaneity or commitment,
A balance between selfish or selfless?

Selfishness allows your heart to be full.
Is it a joy to feel such elation?

Selflessness brings a sadness of unfulfilled hope.
Confusion and disillusion.

Either way, life-changing.

What might be, what might never be.
The outcome was meant to be.

The Mistake.

A choice; head or heart?

A life lesson; perhaps harsh and unpalatable.

A catalyst; multiplies but bringing you closer to home.

A recognition; for the desire to do better.

A smile; for the grounding it creates.

A consideration; for repetition brings no alternative.

A reassurance; increases and resonates, a soothing familiarity.

Right? Wrong? It matters not.

Perfectly imperfect; at peace.

The Surrender.

You can walk through.
An emptiness inside me; a void that can never be
filled.
The physical distance is futile; your presence is
always there.
It keeps on keeping on; always.
There you are, the one who is part of me.

You are always there.
It doesn't fade. It doesn't change. It doesn't
falter.
The potential; replayed often hurts more than
reality.
Time creates a settled sorrow.
There you are, the one who is part of me.

You will never be the same.
A plume that ebbs and flows; the haze always
present.
Choking and gasping amongst the regulations.
Ambiguity or certainty? Perhaps you will never
know.
There you are, the one who is part of me.

The Change.

Will it ever be? I make the change.

I long for the darkness to subside and wait
patiently for hope; an ethereal transcending
white light. Protection.

Gently guiding you down an unfamiliar road;
often one that is uncomfortable and not easily
walked.

I reluctantly pause, I see no change in the
horizon; yet implicitly trust in the way forward.

What if it can never be? The hand of fate deals
with an unfamiliar plan; I let go of expectation.

The road forks; I walk tentatively and
confidently knowing that the road was meant for
me.

Will it ever be? I am the change.

The Alchemist.

The inner voice who speaks the truth,
Fearless against the unknown.
Ushering forward the bold and brave,
whisperings of knowledge feeding the soul.
A desire to absorb and learn,
Embodying the lover, mother, friend, teacher.
The alchemist weaving her enchantment.
Knowing her strength and power she embodies,
The scattering of kindness in recognition for
karma.
Spreading her love far and wide,
Following her heart.
The alchemist weaving her enchantment.
Accepting imperfection,
Always evolving.

The Answer.

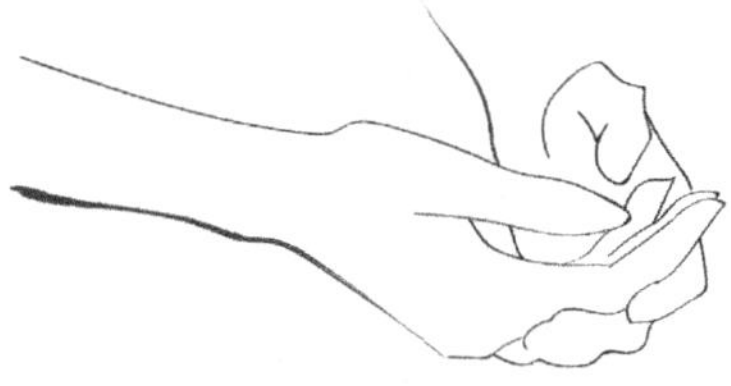

Do you hear me whisper under the masquerade?

The veil lifts, seeking out guidance;
I hear your soft response.

The soothing conversation;
Evoking a veil of confidence.

Your acknowledgement brings clarity.
It resonates and captivates;
the answer I was seeking.

The Light.

I feel the tender warmth of light upon me.
Protecting me in a secure cocoon.

In the tender warmth of light is hope.
Hope will illuminate even the darkest night.

Love is the tender warmth of light.
The tender warmth of light, guiding you
forward.
My eyes close gently and I fade into the idyllic
landscape.
Love is the tender warmth of light.

A heartfelt excitement for the unknown.
Love is what radiates the soul.

In the tender warmth of light and love, a whisper
to follow your heart.
That is where the magic will unfold.

In the tender warmth of light and love your
whole will feel alive!

The Desire.

Dance in the shadows,
Relish in the darkness,
A part you want to hide away.

When your thoughts are less than pure,
That is also where you find you,
Depth and reality.

She will lead with instinct.
Selfish yet honest,
A calling to desire.

The Reflection.

Time for reflection and contemplation.
I look inwards.
The warm hues of summer, a distraction.
Doubt seeps through, fading to cool tones of
change.
Letting go.
My soul moves freely with ease as intuition
guides me.
Calm amidst the chaos.
A force so strong and powerful resonates.
Longing for home.
I am ready.
Approaching a door that is always slightly ajar.
I look inwards.
Is it home? I linger with vigilance.
A hazy yet familiar space beyond.

detached from reality,
a constant cycle of instability.
My logical mind battles with understanding.
It will never be closed but I couldn't stay.
Until the next time.

The Worth.

The pivotal moment comes,
A shattered optimism.
Your heart can take no more.

Torment and turmoil,
Overpowering emotional entrapment.
Enduring cycles of pain.

Repetition must cease,
A new way must prevail,
For sanity and self-worth.

The Release

Escaping the uncertainty,
Peaceful horizon awaits.

Reclaiming power,
Awakening the senses.

Fading towards a whisper,
The deafening subsides.

A shift from tumultuous,
Evaporating into unknown.

Then one day it disappears,
As quickly as it arrived.

Consuming no more,
Never to return.

The Gratitude.

I believed in miracles.
The storm raged ominously.
Darkness.
Rain descended heavily and saturated the
ground.
A kindness that is infectious; spreading far and
wide.
The clouds calmly cleared.
A glistening light surrounds.
Silence.
Water permeating deeply into the earth.
A heartfelt laughter echoes in distance.
The roots spreading their foundation.
The kindness returns.
I believed in me; possibility awaits.
New life emerging effortlessly.
Thankful for the opportunity.
Gratitude for the storm and stability it provided.
Forward was the only way to go.

The Journey.

The darkness lingers,
Motionless, still and silent.

Ever consuming,
Fear fading away.

Awakening the senses,
The shadows subside.

Hope creates the path,
Acceptance of direction.

Navigate forward,
A new sun rises.

Promising fresh beginnings,
Moment passing on.

Transition evolves,
Humbled by enlightenment.
Abundance blossoms.

The Dream.

A feeling that evokes a joy so pure,
An image consistent in mind.
How can that be so wrong?

Desire cares not for situation,
Or passengers on the journey.
It embarks with persistent optimism to reach the
destination.

Determination to make dreams a reality,
What if what you want can never be?
The image touching on delusion.
An inner fire,
Yet the intensity ceases to subside.

Never fully understanding.
But you know,
What is meant for you will be yours.

The Abundance.

As the sun rises creating a golden hue; the gift of possibility presents.
Granted opportunity; a chance to transform.
I am here. I am present.
Resilience through tireless support in battle; cocooned in love.
No resistance.
Joy and coherence in the simple splendours; breathtaking beauty.
No despair.
Courage to thrust forward and empower unknown territories: exceeding expectations.
No fear.
Pleasure embracing the chaos; heart full with love and comfort.
No pain.
Gratitude for the meaningful caress and kind words spoken; genuine adoration.
No sadness.
Calm for creation of reality that needs no escape; unchartered territory and adventure.
No chaos.
I smile a sincere smile; content.
Fortunate beyond measure for the blessings that surround me; a genuine acceptance.
For here I am dancing on the stage of life!

Clarity when I pause, for there it is.
Pure abundance.

The Woman.

Be the energy.

Be the vibe.

Be the kindred spirit.

Be the goddess.

Be the mystery.

Be the adventure.

Be the light.

Be the darkness.

Be the joy.

Be the power.

Be the wisdom.

Be you.

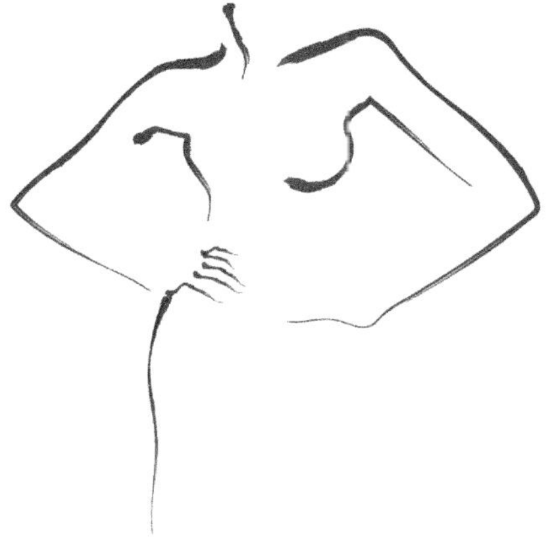